The Nikola Tesla Story

Margaret Storm

PART V

The Nikola Tesla Story

Nikola Telsa was not an earth man. The space people have stated that a male child was born on board a space ship which was on a flight from Venus to the earth in July, 1856. The little boy was called Nikola. The ship landed at midnight, between July 9 and 10, in a remote mountain province in what is now Yugoslavia. There, according to arrangements, the child was placed in the care of a good man and his wife, the Rev. Milutin and Djouka Telsa.

The space people released this information in 1947 to Arthur H. Matthews of Quebec, Canada, an electrical engineer who from boyhood was closely associated with Tesla.

In 1944, a year after the death of Tesla, the late John J. O'Neill, then science editor of the *New York Herald Tribune*, wrote an excellent story of Tesla's life and work, en-

71

titled *Prodigal Genius*. As a reporter O'Neill frequently interviewed Tesla and had the greatest respect for the superman. But O'Neill lacked the occult understanding necessary to correctly interpret the extraordinary powers which set Tesla apart from this world. O'Neill made the common error of assuming that Tesla had died as do ordinary mortals: that his work was finished, and that he left no disciples.

O'Neill could not have been more mistaken. In the first place Tesla was not a mortal according to earth standards: being a Venusian he is now able to work on earth in his subtle body with far greater facility than when in his physical body. Tesla carefully trained certain disciples to continue his physical plane work under his supervision after he had shed his physical body.

He entrusted Arthur H. Matthews of Canada with many tasks, at least two of which are of vital current interest — the Tesla interplanetary communications set and the Tesla anti-war machine.

Mr. Matthews built a model Tesla set for interplanetary communications in 1947 and has operated it successfully since. However, he has tuned in only on space ships thus far, for the set has a limited range. He is now engaged in building a more elaborate set, and will be able to speak more freely of it since he is incorporating many of his own inventive ideas in it. The original design was given to him in confidence by Tesla and he naturally does not intend to violate that confidence.

Mr. Matthews has the complete design for the anti-war machine ready and waiting for any nation which has the courage to use it. Tesla designed the anti-war machine in 1935 but Mr. Matthews has worked on it constantly since, incorporating in it many major improvements.

Another disciple who was specially trained by Tesla is Otis T. Carr of Baltimore, Maryland. Carr has recently invented free-energy devices capable of powering anything from a hearing aid to a spaceship. Carr was studying art in New York and working in a hotel package room to support himself. Tesla, who was not only completely telepathic but also in touch with the Christ Forces on the Inner Planes, lived in the hotel where Carr was employed. Telsa came straight to his young disciple, asked him to buy four pounds of unsalted peanuts and deliver them to his suite. From this beginning Carr was trained by Tesla over a period of three years in almost daily conversations that always started with the peanut delivery. The peanuts were for the New York pigeons which Tesla so loved.

The remarkable achievements of both Matthews and Carr are covered in later chapters of this book. But it may be said here that Tesla is in no sense a disembodied spirit seeking to communicate with disciples and guiding them from the astral plane. Mediums who engage, for profit of course, in receiving messages from the astral plane have tried with vim and with vigor to drum up trade via the spirit or ghost of Tesla. But Tesla is not a ghost, nor did he stand a ghost of a chance of being a ghost. Tesla was an Adept, an Initiate, a Venusian. He was at all times earth-free; he was never earthbound.

Naturally Tesla did not go around bragging about these matters. But when he did meet up with a server of the Light Tesla lost no time in engaging in a good talkfest. Both Matthews and Carr have carried out Tesla's work since 1943 without the slightest difficulty. When asked how best to approach the work of Tesla, how to understand his discoveries, both Matthews and Carr have a standard answer. If you wish to understand Tesla you must attune your mind to God.

Tesla and his Twin Ray, the White Dove who was his constant companion on earth, are now working in the scientific department of Shamballa, and they do overshadow disciples. But it should be clearly understood that this overshadowing process, when conducted by an Initiate, is in no sense related to any type of psychism or mediumship. Every Initiate overshadows disciples; otherwise there would be no point in evolution if the higher energies could not in some manner direct lower energies. Every Initiate must have disciples in the world of form. Disciples are called upon to operate typewriters, design machinery and do all the other chores of the workaday world. A disciple is an outpost of consciousness for an Adept.

What, the reader might ask, is the oustanding characteristic which distinguishes a Tesla disciple? In every case a Tesla disciple is, consciously or unconsciously, affiliated with one or more of the Masters of Wisdom, and is a student in a Master's Ashram, although this fact may be known only on the Inner Planes. Every Tesla disciple is working with the energies from at least five cosmic Rays, and is usually unconscious of his correct Ray status as knowledge of this kind can easily become a source of pride and therefore a handicap. Every Tesla disciple extends the hand of friendship to our interplanetary neighbors. Every Tesla disciple is already firmly oriented in the New Age and has unbounded enthusiasm for a free and joyous world.

Many persons who worked for Tesla, or who were associated with him closely as was John J. O'Neill, have expressed disappointment that Tesla did not leave a heritage of great scientific secrets which could be explored, and, of course.

exploited. But, Tesla, the Venusian, had no secrets. Only earth people are greedy enough and stupid enough to have secrets.

The Venusians, Martians, and visitors from other planets who fly through the earth's atmosphere daily, have no secrets either. They have a message: Love ye one another. But earth people have successfully ignored that message for at least 2,000 years, and they might go right on ignoring it save for New Age developments based on application of universal Law. Such application was the clue to all of Tesla's achievements. He was a discoverer, not a mere inventor.

There seem to be no records of Tesla revealing his identity as a Venusian during his earth life. But when the announcement of this fact was made to Mr. Matthews by the space people it did not come as a surprise in most quarters, because by then it was generally known that at least ten million people from other planets had been infiltrated into the earth's population. It had long been known that most of the Masters of Wisdom, down through the centuries, were volunteers from other worlds. But it seemed doubtful, for a time, that Tesla himself, had been personally aware of his origin during his physical plane life on earth.

However, it now appears that he did understand his mission which was actually to prepare the planet earth for the space age. The fact that he told Otis T. Carr so much about other planets indicates that he was quite familiar with the subject. He frankly told Carr that he, Carr, was destined to explore space. Tesla also gave Mr. Matthews the design for the interplanetary communications set in 1938, another clear indication that Tesla knew that other planets were inhabited. and he obviously knew they possessed spaceships. He told Mr. Matthews that the set should be built in a few years after 1938, at which time spaceships from other worlds would approach the earth.

Tesla never married, and never had any romantic attachments or even close friendships with either men or women, except in certain cases where the bond was one of discipleship or where some useful purpose would be served for the benefit of humanity. Tesla not only lived alone in hotels, but he lived behind locked doors. Only occasionally was a maid permitted to enter his room to clean it. However, Otis T. Carr, over a period of three years, was his daily visitor and Tesla explained to Carr that visitors were not normally allowed because, coming into his suite from the harsh, outside world, they immediately lowered the vibrations in the rooms in which Tesla had to live and work and commune with his Creator.

Mr. Carr has explained that often, when he came to Tesla's suite, bringing the four pounds of unsalted peanuts, Tesla would ask him to just sit down and relax for an hour or more. Not a word would be spoken between the two men. Yet when Carr rose to leave he would feel refreshed and inspired. The vibrations in the room had done the necessary work, attuning and purifying his four lower bodies.

Tesla had another trusted friend in the person of Boris De Tanko, a New York publisher. Mr. De Tanko has related how, Saturday after Saturday, he used to meet Tesla for luncheon at the old Hotel Brevoort on lower Fifth Avenue, a place famous for its fine French cuisine. Mr. De Tanko always found these luncheon visits highly inspiring, though unusual in some respects. He said that often the two of them sat together at the table in complete silence for well over an hour; finally Tesla would speak and then the illuminating conversation would flow like molten gold.

Both Mr. Matthews and Mr. Carr received from Tesla a
eat deal of confidential information about future world
nditions and developments concerning the emergence of
e New Age civilization. Most of this information had to do
ith space, with space ships, space people, and interplanetary
mmunications.

When Tesla shed his physical body in 1943, it was ap-
rent that he was leaving the physical plane of manifest ap-
arances to enter into more subtle vibrations; vibrations
hich were invisible to the average man. These vibrations
ere not invisible to Tesla; he was completely clairvoyant,
airaudient and telepathic, as is any Adept. Again it must
e stressed that this type of clarity has nothing whatever to
o with mediumship or psychism. The latter belongs to the
nimal kingdom. Tesla was never really at home on the
hysical plane, dealing with matter in its harshest state: in
e subtle worlds he was completely free. Yet for 87 of the
ost difficult years ever visited upon this planet Tesla cared on his work like the great gentlemen he was.

In retrospect the pattern of his physical sojourn in the
orld of form, which seemed so complex to writers like
ohn J. O'Neill, emerges in simple clarity. Tesla had ob-
iously agreed to come to the earth as a volunteer worker
o assist in launching the New Age which he knew to be
ynonymous with the Space Age. It is perfectly apparent that
scended Master Saint Germain had to bring in people from
ther planets, people with knowledge of outer space condi-
ions, to handle the major aspects of the planned program.

Tesla was designated to work on the third Ray of Love-in-
Action, for that is the Ray which supplies our atmosphere
vith electricity. The first three major Rays form the three
spects of God as defined by major religions; the four minor

Rays provide what we recognize as God's attributes. Christianity correctly defines the first three Rays as a Trinity, representing the Father, the Son, and the Holy Spirit.

The first or Father aspect is derived from the Ray of Power and Purpose; the second, the Son or sun aspect, is the Ray of Illumination and Wisdom leading to Intelligent Love-in-Action, or the third Ray. Originally, we were all Sons of God or Sparks from the Great Central Sun of the galaxy. From the strictly scientific point of view the first three Rays provide life, light, and electricity to this planet.

The fourth Ray of Purity leads man through conflict to harmony. The fifth Ray is that of concrete science and knowledge and provides the world of form with an understandable functional basis. The sixth Ray energizes all of man's ideals and ideologies, whether wise or foolish. During the Piscean Age it led to the rise of Christianity and churchianity, and to all sorts of experimental economic and political systems. Then follows the seventh Ray, now in manifestation; the Ray which is now being called into action to transmute and release mankind from all past errors accumulated during nineteen million years of struggle since the laggards came.

At the present time, and for centuries past, all individuals who desired so-called occult knowledge have been regularly taken into the various Ray Temples or Retreats for training at night while the physical body lies sleeping. The Temples are open twenty-four hours a day round the globe so their facilities are always available to students. It should not be considered that this training is mystical; it is strictly utilitarian and practical and is designed to make physical plane living easier and more wholesome. It is designed to lead not to death, but to the Ascension for each individual.

For example, every great musical composer down through the ages has been a Temple student. Some composers are able to bring through their memories with greater accuracy than others. Wagner was an outstanding student in the Music Temple, and during his waking hours he was able to bring through musical notations with scarcely a deviation from the original Temple teachings. The story of Lohengrin is one of his finest examples.

It is presumed that Tesla not only had the usual free access to the Temples during his sleeping hours, but that he also had direct communication while in full waking consciousness. This is not unusual for even an advanced student; it is the normal practice for Initiates. In the outer world there is no information available on Tesla's exact evolutionary status on Venus, but it is known that the entire Venusian race is considered adept from our point of view. However, when space people take earth bodies they are often mercifully granted certain mental blockages for their own protection. That is, if a Venusian had a full and complete memory of his life on Venus, he would find it well nigh impossible to cope daily with earth situations. Even the Initiate Jesus did not have a complete mental grasp of His true mission until He was more than twelve years of age. It was then that He was taken to India for personal training under the supervision of His great teacher, the Christ, known in the outer world as Lord Maitreya.

John J. O'Neill has written a most detailed story of Tesla's life and scientific work in *Prodigal Genius*. But for those readers who are just becoming oriented in this field of study, it might be well to pause here for a brief review of the highlights that lighted the path of the man who came to earth to

bring electricity to our homes and factories and illumina
to our darkened minds.

Historians agree that Nikola Tesla was born at midni
between July 9 and 10, in the year of 1856. Nikola him
hinted on a few occasions that this was not the date of
birth. These hints were disregarded along with hundreds
other statements made by Tesla, because in most quart
he was regarded as being a bit impractical. This was no
criticism, for his genius was so highly respected that it
generally conceded that he did not have to measure up
conventional standards. He was to be allowed his little
centricities, his passing fancies. The space people have n
stated that Nikola was born on board their ship on a fli
from Venus, and that they landed on the earth at midnig
between July 9 and 10, 1856.

When the space people say that Nikola was *born* on boa
one of their ships, they do not mean that it was a physi
birth. Physical conception and the birthing processes kno
on this planet are not used elsewhere. A sex system was
troduced here after the laggards came, in order to keep t
race in manifestation, and to provide for re-embodiment
groups bound by karma. This allowed karmic debts to
paid off in kind under the old law of "an eye for an ey
and a tooth for a tooth." On other planets positive and neg
tive light rays are used to produce a physical form whi
can be occupied by an evolving lifestream. The form is
full stature. It is only on this planet that tiny, baby forn
are utilized.

Djouka Tesla, the earth mother who cared for Nikola with a rare tenderness, was a most remarkable woman and assuredly possessed advanced spiritual powers. It has been said that she, too, was a Venusian, and if this is true, it accounts for her very unusual abilities. She was the eldest child in a family of seven children. Her father was a minister of the Serbian Orthodox Church. Her mother had become blind after the seventh child was born and Djouka unhesitatingly took charge of the entire household. She never attended school, nor did she learn even the rudiments of reading and writing at home. Yet she moved with ease in cultured circles as did her family. Here was a woman who could neither read nor write, yet she possessed literary abilities far beyond those of a person of considerable education.

Tesla, himself, never wearied of talking about his remarkable mother, and described how she had absorbed "by ear" all the cultural riches of her community and her nation. Like Nikola, she apparently had the power of instant recall. Nikola said that she could easily recite, without error, long passages from the Bible; she could repeat thousands of versus of the national poetry of her country. It was because of her great interest in poetry that Nikola, in his busy American days as a superman, still found time to translate and have published some of the best examples of Serbian sagas.

His mother was also famed throughout her home provinces for her artistic ability, often expressed in beautiful needlework. She possessed remarkable manual dexterity, and Nikola said her fingers were so sensitive that she could tie three knots in an eyelash—even when she was past sixty years of age.

She had an excellent grasp of philosophy and apparently

a practical understanding of mechanical and technical devices. She needed a loom for household weaving, so she designed and built one. She did not think of herself as an inventor, yet she built many labor-saving devices and in-
struments for her household. In addition she was so skillful
in handling business and financial matters that she managed
all accounts for her household as well as for her husband's
church.

Nikola's earth father was the son of an army officer, and
as a young man set out on a military career. But he was
soon disillusioned for he was irked by the discipline, and
turned to his true calling in the literary field. He wrote
poetry, articles on current problems, and philosophical es-
says. This led, quite naturally, to the ministry, giving him
an opportunity to write sermons and to speak from the
pulpit. He did not limit himself to the usual church topics,
but ranged far and wide, covering subjects of local and national interest concerning labor, social and economic problems. Until Nikola was seven years of age, the father had a
parish church at Smiljan, an agricultural community in a
high plateau region in that part of the Alps which stretch
from Switzerland to Greece.

This then was the childhood environment of the boy from
Venus. It was a life filled with joy. He had an ideal home
with a loving understanding family. He lived in a magnificent countryside, close to nature. He was a boy like other
little boys up to a certain point, the point at which he became
the superboy, foreshadowing the superman. And so it was
that he lacked human companions, a state, not of loneliness
but of aloneness, that was to continue throughout his physical
incarnation. The unlighted ones whom he met everywhere
through the years felt sorry for him because they assumed

he was lonely. Tesla never tried to explain his position for he knew he would meet with no understanding from an alien world. To the end of his time in a physical body he lived at the very center, the very core, of a magnificent solitude, listening always to the Voice of the Silence.

As a boy Nikola liked nothing better than to wander in the woods and over the mountains near his home. His little friends did not understand or share his boundless enthusiasm for trees, streams, birds and their nests, sunshine, clouds and stormy skies. Nor did they enjoy what they considered the hard work connected with Nikola's many boyhood inventions. He was constantly engaged in experiments that often failed, a fact which made them all the more fascinating. In reviewing his life in later years, he could look back upon these many lines of investigation which he had started as a boy and see how they led directly to some of his major inventions.

As he grew to maturity he displayed certain characteristics which might have revealed his Venusian origin had they been understood. His hands were unusually long, particularly his thumbs, and were extremely sensitive, carrying strong clean etheric currents. Inasmuch as he was clairvoyant he could easily see the murky gray astral matter which exudes from the hands of the ordinary person, an effluvia of filth so sticky that it will adhere to the etheric structure of another person—even an individual occupying a body of high vibrations.

For this reason Tesla always dreaded shaking hands. He tried to avoid such contacts even at the cost of being thought inconsiderate or impolite. On occasion, when it was absolutely necessary for him to shake hands with certain visitors in his New York office, he escaped at the earliest possible moment to his private washroom where he thoroughly washed his hands, drying them on a clean towel which was handed to him by his secretary and used only once.

He had the deep-set piercing eyes of the Initiate, clear blue in color. He also breathed correctly, something an earth person seldom achieves. This was a natural faculty, for as a small child he discovered that by breathing deeply he was overcome by a feeling of lightness in his body. He felt so weightless that he concluded he would be able to fly if he developed the will to do so. It is said that he did not know he was unusual in this respect while he was still a child. Tesla could leave his body at will when he grew older. He always lived in hotels, and his orders were that he was never to be disturbed in his locked room. Tesla used projected consciousness as do all Initiates, although this is not to be confused with the type of astral projection practiced by the average person. The Initiate uses many types of etheric energies freely and in a manner which is always spiritually correct. The ordinary individual does not have the ability to utilize these energies or even to contact them, and therefore easily falls into the dangerous practice of using astral or lower mental forces. This leads to the next step on the left-hand path—the state of trance mediumship.

When Tesla was a small boy and found that his rhythmic breathing gave him a feeling that he could fly, he quite naturally and normally began to practice levitation. In this is a profound lesson for all of us, and it is the same lesson that Jesus stressed. Jesus warned us that we should not accept appearances, if those appearances might prove limiting to us. We are always imitating that which we see about us. We see people growing old, so we grow old. If everyone thought of growing younger, and youth began to manifest all about us, we would grow younger in appearance as a matter of course. We see people walking, so we walk. Young Nikola saw people walking, but he knew in his heart that it was a cumbersome and laborious method, so he pondered over it and got the *feeling* that he could fly. Then he followed his own inner *feeling;* not the example set by appearances all about him. He rose from the earth, levitated, and moved through space freely.

It might have startled unsuspecting New Yorkers to see Tesla take off like his companion, the White Dove, and fly over the city. But those who understand levitation and use it can also throw a cloak of invisibility about themselves. People jumped to strange conclusions about what they thought were the eccentricities of a great scientist. Another great One by the name of Jesus walked on water, and the curious are still talking about it today. Tesla well knew that it was the better part of wisdom to remain invisible when he had his feet off the ground, so to speak.

Some of his close associates knew that he could levitate and respected the confidence. It might be well to underscore a point here—the person who levitates by using his Christ Principle to do so, must have a purpose behind his action, and it must be a purpose which is in some way furthering the Divine Plan. It is not spiritually permissible to levitate merely as a form of entertainment, for oneself or for others. Levitation is correctly used only if one is definitely going somewhere for a definite reason in the service of humanity. The average individual moves according to his own whim and pleasure, and usually to satisfy some personal objective which is often unnecessary. The average person moves about because of restlessness and an inherent inability to work according to any plan, let alone the Divine Plan.

The limitations of walking have offered certain advantages
in the past. Transportation was so difficult that people tended
to remain quiet as much as possible, or if they did go on a
walking journey they often utilized the time to commune
with nature or their fellowmen. But the advent of the auto-
mobile, bus, plane, and train, has introduced a method of
transportation which adds only noise, confusion and chaos
to the general picture; and which constantly exposes the
emotional body to jarring impacts of a most distressing
sort.

When Nikola was five years of age, he designed and installed a waterwheel across a mountain brook near his home
at Smiljan. He utilized a disk cut from a tree trunk by lum-
ber workers, some small branches, sticks and rocks. The
device was a wonderful success from the standpoint of the
young inventor. It was a bit crude, but it rotated. He had
used the methods of antiquity in designing his model and
it was only much later that he discovered that waterwheels
have paddles, but his wheel operated without paddles.

This waterwheel was his first demonstration of a lesson
he never forgot—to utilize free energy which was being
constantly and freely replaced by Nature. Later, perhaps as
a direct result of this experiment as a five-year-old boy, he
developed the smooth-disk turbine. Later, too, he carried
his experiments in utilizing the free energy of Nature into
the atmosphere, and there he found that electricity in unlimited abundance would give him unlimited power—free
energy that would carry mankind itself to freedom from the

great curse of grueling labor. This was Tesla's magnificent concept that dominated his every thought as an inventor— free energy for a free world. It was the concept that carried him to the heights of cosmic fellowship, and the one mighty flame of inspiration which he set before his disciples as an eternal beacon—free energy to make and keep the people free.

When he was nine years old, he designed his first motor. It was made from tiny pieces of wood and shaped somewhat like a windmill. But it was not powered by the wind. It was powered by June bugs, flying round and round, trying to detach their feet from the glue which held them fast to their duties.

An incident took place at this time which clearly indicated the clean and wholesome trend of Tesla's thinking. He used June bugs because he needed to somehow capture power from the air although the bugs might have been happier had they not been drafted for this service. But Nikola used bugs just as a plowman would use horses. However, a little companion came in to observe the motor. He spied a reserve supply of June bugs which Nikola had placed in a small jar and the child grabbed a handful of the bugs and ate them. Nikola was so sickened by the event that he set the remaining bugs free and never again utilized bug-power. This was his first direct step toward capturing power from the air without enslavement of animal or human labor.

It was also at this time, when he was finishing his elementary studies and entering the Gymnasium for more advanced school work, that he first came to grips with his occult power of working in the fourth ether. He had only to think of an object, and it would appear before him, exhibiting the normal appearance of mass, solidity and dimensions.

He had discussed this matter in confidence with his mother, for he found the ability to be a nuisance rather than an asset and wished to be rid of it.

Whether or not his mother could explain it was never revealed; now in retrospect it seems that she herself probably possessed the same power and understood it thoroughly. But Nikola was still a child and his mother agreed with him that he should attempt to banish the visions if he wished. From the occult point of view this was the correct thing to do, for no adult person should ever try to influence a child or tamper with a child's efforts to come to grips with spiritual realities. This kind of tampering has proved to be the great curse of churchianity and one of the most dangerous of black magic practices.

A little later Nikola confided to his mother that he wished to keep and use the power to envision objects before him, but that he wished to bring it under complete control. Again his mother agreed with him. The power to work in the fourth ether—a psysical substance which forms the plane of density just a little finer than gas—is a power possessed in full by every advanced Initiate. They also work freely in the third, second and first ethers, which together with the lower four—physical, liquid, gaseous and the fourth ether— form the seven ethers which comprise the entire plane of of matter. Scientists have not worked with the ethers because they could not see them, and it is not generally realized that the dense physical plane is only concretized ether. There is nothing mystical about working in the finer ethers; in fact, it is a scientific shortcut. There is actually no reason to dig gold out of the earth and then process it. It is much easier to extract it from the ether and precipitate it on to the physical plane. But in an earlier chapter of this book it was explained that after the laggards came man lost his power to precipitate matter, for he lost the use of the Rays. It was only then that man started digging in the soil and extracting his needs from the lowest plane of matter.

Today on the Inner Planes where the Lords of Karma work. the whole plan for re-embodiment has been changed to bring it into line with needs for the New Age civilization. Greater selectivity is practiced and many children are now being born who have the ability to work in the fourth ether as did Nikola Tesla. Therefore. the whole subject is one which should be thoroughly explored by scientists, teachers and parents, if these adults wish to understand New Age children and participate in the civilization which they will produce.

It has been stated by the Spiritual Hierarchy that within 300 years the entire race will be telepathic and will possess etheric vision. These are natural human unfoldments following the normal course of evolution which is now being guided on the physical plane once again by the Hierarchy. The race is moving forward in evolution in a manner of speaking. but at the same time we are striving to get back to a point at which we stood nineteen million years ago. It is that point that each of us must attain during the Aquarian Age. Then from that point each will move forward swiftly toward the Ascension and go on to new evolutionary assignments on other stars.

At this particular time, it is most essential that the general public become informed about etheric vision and telepathy, for there is much dangerous confusion on the subject. This is planned confusion, engineered down to the last degree by the forces of darkness. Such confusion does not exist in the minds of those who are serving the Light. It exists in the

minds of the bewildered masses because of their inability
to exercise discrimination. They listen to the press, the
preachers and the teachers, and swallow whatever happens
to appeal to their basic desire nature. Thus do the dark
forces brainwash the masses into a lethargic state of docil-
ity: the masses follow along like sheep to the slaughter.

The powers possessed by Nikola Tesla were in no sense
psychic powers. The ability to see into the fourth ether, to
mold the etheric substance into machinery as did Tesla, and
then to test that etheric machinery and make any necessary
adjustments as did Tesla—all of this has nothing whatever
to do with the astral plane. The astral plane is man-made.
Astral matter is filthy matter. Tesla struck right through
the astral plane and had no contact with it. As Arthur H.
Matthews has truly stated: When Tesla wanted something
he went straight to God.

In these dangerous times that advice is the best possible—
when we want something we should go straight to God and
talk to Him about it. Today there are hundreds if not mil-
lions of people who have responded to ancient decadent Atlantean vibrations. The reason for this is because certain
sections of the submerged continent are to be brought up in
the very near future. When Atlantis went down three cities
were sealed. These cities will soon be brought up to the sur-
face of the Atlantic and will be used as exhibits of Atlantean
culture. This is one of the projects which is being handled
by the angelic kingdom under the direction of Saint Germain
in His capacity as Lord of Civilization.

The response to ancient Atlantean vibrations is a dangerous response. Human beings mistakenly feel that the ability
to see into astral matter is a sign of the advanced Initiate.
An Initiate possesses powers which enable him to stand on

this earth and yet observe incidents on Venus or Mars. He can also look out over the earth and sweep the entire scene with one glance. He can look through the earth and watch activities within the dense physical globe.

Thus it will be realized that the Initiate is completely free. He can see above, as below. The person with astral vision is a prisoner of his own limited and highly questionable power. If he has the ability to see auras, colors, and so forth, what of it? Usually he uses the power merely to satisfy personal curiosity in exactly the same way that he uses the power of speech to indulge in gossip. When an Initiate looks out over the universe you may be certain that He has some excellent reason for doing so. He may carefully inspect the aura of a disciple in order to determine the corrections needed. He may inspect the aura of a great city to determine the spiritual strength of the populace, but along the way He does not stop to watch a football game or look over the latest bargains in the shopping marts. On the other hand, the person with astral vision is not only subject to normal distractions of physical eyesight, but he is subjected to the constant nervous impact of additional colors, movements and so forth.

Peace of mind and serenity of soul do not lie along that route; nor can the Voice of the Silence be heard within the beating heart of the unlighted ones who amuse themselves with such nonsense. Astral vision is more often a sign of regression than of advancement, for it simply denotes the attainment of certain animal characteristics. It must be remembered that all animals in certain advanced groups—dogs, cats, horses and elephants—have astral vision. Many other animals also possess it and most animals are telepathic within certain limits.

In humans, this type of clairvoyance is often associated with solar plexus telepathy, another animal characteristic. Many persons who use solar plexus telepathy are inclined to confuse it with mental telepathy, and those who practice mental telepathy are frequently unaware that the only type of telepathy which can be considered as a spiritual power is from Soul to Soul, or from Ascended-Master to Soul. The Soul referred to here is the I AM Presence Who overshadows us, or the Christ-Self Who abides in the heart Flame.

Individuals who strive to cultivate their astral abilities, even though they may be born with them, are following an extremely dangerous course, and one which can lead easily from psychism to black magic and from black magic to insanity. If an individual is born with psychic powers he should either banish them at all costs, or he should take up the proper study which will enable him to serve the Forces of Light to the limit of his capacity. These astral conditions are karmic, but if properly channeled they can lead to discipleship. If they are not properly channeled, they can and will lead only to mediumship and misery.

Mediumship is the way of retrogression. Discipleship is the way to the path of truth, light, beauty and unlimited cosmic freedom. Every individual has only one rule to follow and this is it: Place yourself at all times under the full power and protection of your own God-Presence, your Christ-Self or Soul, for your own Higher Self is your first and best teacher. There is no need to be running around the Himalayas or elsewhere searching for a guru or Master. When you are ready to be of service to the Hierarchy your own Master, and He will be an Ascended Master, will seek you out—intuitively, of course, not physically—and you will not have to worry about being kept busy in the service of the Light. There is plenty to do.

It is the Soul or Christ-Self that comes into incarnation, not the physical body or the emotions or the lower concrete mind. The Soul builds these lower vehicles for convenience, and in accordance with the pattern of karma carried over from previous embodiments. Therefore, the Soul should at all times be permitted to train and use the lower vehicles according to the purpose designated in the Divine Plan.

The part which Nikola Tesla was to play in the Divine Plan unfolded quickly when he enrolled at the Gymnasium at Gospic, a large town to which his father had been assigned as a minister. He discovered that his favorite subject was mathematics. So intense was his devotion to this study that his teachers had to overlook his loathing for freehand drawing. It was thought that Nikola was unhappy about drawing because he was left-handed at that time. Eventually he became ambidextrous, another mark of the Initiate.

Many years later it was clearly demonstrated that Nikola loathed drawing because he could work in the fourth ether so easily, designing and building his machines in etheric substance, testing them and making necessary adjustments in the ether, and then leaving them "on file" in the ether. For him drawing was utterly unrealistic and an unmitigated nuisance. He did not have to make plans and jot down dimensions, because of his power of instant recall. After designing a machine in etheric substance he might have no occasion to think of it again for a period of five years or

so. Yet when he did need the design he could call it up
stantly before him, complete with exact dimensions.

In the school at Gospic Nikola first came to desire to I
this power which he had possessed since birth, but he also
sired to bring it under full control and use it, rather t
allow it to use him and enslave him. Nikola had no wisl
be submerged in paper work, even in his schooldays
thought which might be of value to many business :
government executives today.

Nikola found that he did not need to go to the bla
board in the classroom to work out a problem. At
thought of "blackboard" it appeared in the ether bef
him. As the problem was stated it appeared instantly on
etheric blackboard together with all the symbols and ope
tions required to work out the solution. Each step appea
instantly, and much more rapidly than anyone could p
sibly work out the problem on paper or slate. Therefc
by the time the whole problem had been stated, Nik
could give the solution immediately.

At first his teachers thought he was just an extrem
clever boy who had found some method of cheating. Ho
ever, in a short time they were forced to admit that no
ception could possibly be practiced, so they gladly accep
the glamor shed abroad as the rumor got around that
Gospic classroom was graced by a genius. Nikola ne
bothered to explain about the etheric blackboard for
intuitively knew that he would be casting pearls. Alwa
through the passing years he guarded his power as the gr
spiritual treasure he knew it to be.

He used the same power to replace all customary memo
functions, and he soon discovered that he could learn forei
languages with little of the usual effort. He became proficie

in German, French and Italian in those early years, and this
opened up to him entire new worlds that remained closed
to other students. His father's library contained hundreds of
fine books and by the time Nikola was eleven years old he
had read them all. He had little in common with his school-
mates, and, in fact, little in common with his teachers. But
they accepted him because he was a lovable lad without a
trace of arrogance or pride. But neither did he shroud himself in an exaggerated sense of humility. He was a normal,.
natural friendly boy living in a natural, friendly world.

On fine summer days he would often wander over the
mountains from Gospic to sit again beside the brook at
Smiljin, and watch his little waterwheel in operation—the
wheel he had designed and installed at the age of five years.
He was constantly working on mechanical devices during
the years he was in school at Gospic, but the school offered
no courses that could help him—not even a course in manual
training.

However, he did bring into focus one decision that fore-
shadowed the superman. The school on one occasion arranged an exhibit of models of waterwheels. They were not
working models but Nikola could easily envision them in full
action. In his home hung a picture which he had often carefully studied. His father explained that it was a picture of
Niagara Falls in America.

In school, Nikola looked at the model waterwheels. At
home he gazed again at the picture of Niagara Falls. Filled
with prophetic joy he exultantly turned to his father and
said: "Someday I am going to America and harness
Niagara Falls for power". Thirty years later he carried out
his plan, exactly as he had predicted it at the age of ten
years.

Two other experiments which he worked on during these childhood years proved to be starting points for mature inventions. He discovered that air leaking into a vacuum produced a small amount of rotation in a cylinder. This was not the result he had intended, but he accepted it, and many, many years later, it led to his invention of the Tesla turbine, or what he called a "powerhouse in a hat" because it broke all records for horsepower developed per pound of weight.

The other experiment has not been carried out to its final conclusion, but now that Tesla has shed his physical body, he is working on it from the Inner Planes. In some form it will be presented as a New Age development under the general heading of weather control. While wandering in the mountains one day a thunderstorm broke overhead, and Nikola saw the lightning flash and then saw the rain come down in torrents. He reasoned that the lightning had produced the downpour.

Scientists, years later, argued that high up in the air the rain had come first, and the lightning followed. The raindrops fell slowly to earth, while the lightning flash was observed in a fraction of a second. But Tesla somehow knew that if he could produce lightning he could control the the weather.

He never placed any limits on his thinking and even while walking over the mountains, through the downpour, he envisioned the day when rain could be produced when and where needed, thus providing an abundant food supply the world round. He never lost this vision, and thirty years later, in the mountains of Colorado, he produced bolts of lightning. He planned to use such bolts in his rain-making device but was stopped by the United States Patent Office which refused to go along with his invention.

Now it can be readily seen that his invention might have been premature. For both rain and lightning are produced by the activities of the angelic kingdom. The water devas, fire devas and wind devas serve as housekeepers in the atmosphere around the planet. When they wish to wash out a certain section of the atmosphere, they produce as much rain as they need, and shoot bolts of lightning through the skies to counteract poisonous astral accumulations. The amount of rain that happens to fall on the ground depends entirely upon how much scrubbing is being done up yonder. When the scrub pails are emptied the rain stops.

The devas are not charged with duties such as going around with watering pots for the purpose of irrigating gardens. That problem is in the human province. The devas are very responsive and can be called into action by invocation; or when enough water has been sprinkled and floods threaten they can be stopped by invocation. Human beings should be trained to recognize their own karmic results and do something intelligent about it instead of moaning about the weather. All weather conditions can be under human control. Noah tackled that problem and took the steps necessary to deal with it. Then he sent forth the dove from the ark, and the dove returned with a plucked olive leaf, the symbol of peaceful waters subsiding from the flooded lands. But the dove cannot return unless people first send the dove forth.

When Tesla walked through the rainstorm he was witnessing angelic activities, even though he might not have thought of the matter in quite that way. But he knew that somehow his true work belonged up there in space, high above the mountains of earth. He knew that all worthwhile works must start at the Source. He knew that if he could

understand the wonders of flashing lightning and streaming
rain then weather could be mechanically controlled. He was
correct, for while weather can be controlled through human
invocation to the angels, it can also be controlled by a
mechanical device. This will be another scientific revelation
of the New Age: another proof that the old nonsensical
concepts concerning mysticism must go, along with the old
concepts about floods and droughts.

Nikola had distinguished himself as a scholar at the age
of fourteen. That was in the year of 1870, and his schooldays at Gospic were over. He was a sensitive lad, highly
intuitive, alert to the constancy of angels and the stupidities
of men. His strength was actually extraordinary, for he
often read and studied the whole night through, attended his
classes by day, and completed a vast educational program of
his own outside school hours. But because of his extreme
sensitivity, his slim build, and his fastidious nature that
demanded a degree of cleanliness far beyond the call of duty,
his father felt that the boy was in delicate health.

His father was determined to protect him, and as it turned
out the protective attitude paid dividends a few years later
when Nikola was spared compulsory military duty because
his father was convinced that his delicate son would never
survive army life. Nikola, in accord with his father's carefully planned arrangements, was forced to hide out in the
mountains for more than a year while apparently attempting
to recover his health. During this time his father was able
to make certain contacts among the military, so that his son's
absence was conveniently overlooked.

Nikola himself found military duty a subject so loathsome
that he could not even bring himself to think about it. Intuitively he knew he would never serve in the army, so he

made the most of his year of mountain solitude, and returned to his home in good health and with his head filled with scientific plans that, if carried out, probably would have proved earth-shaking in a most literal way.

But all this took place when he reached military age. His first serious difficulties started in 1870 when he finished school at Gospic. Because of his sensitive nature, his father felt that he should not continue his studies, but should go directly into the ministry. His scholarship at the age of fourteen was sufficiently outstanding to equip him to serve in the church.

So far as Nikola was concerned the church was as bad as the army, and, in fact, worse, for the army was still some distance in the future but the church was at hand. Moreover, he had already decided on university training in electrical engineering, and was a dedicated disciple anxious to be about his Father's business in the cosmos. When an individual of the spiritual stature of Tesla comes into incarnation nothing is allowed to interfere with the purpose outlined on the Inner Planes. Plans for the embodiment are carefully arranged in accordance with the Divine Plan for the whole project under development. Initiates work with a high degree of spiritual efficiency. Certain universal needs are scheduled which must be met within time limits by certain disciples appointed to the task, and all of these plans must dovetail according to a certain pre-determined pattern.

At this particular point Nikola had to be saved from a career in the church. The point could not be argued, especially between parents and a 14-year-old boy. Moreover, under Law the free will of the family members had to be permitted full sway; between the three of them they had to come to free will decision, but at the same time the decision had to be the correct one. Free will is somewhat paradoxical in any case, but especially so in the case of disciples. That is why discipleship is always fraught with extreme difficulty. The disciple is called upon to make a decision, and yet he must make the correct one which stands upon the Inner Planes, and he must meet a time schedule. But happily a way is always provided, though it may be a way of severe struggle.

In the case of Nikola it was the way of psychic illness and was far from pleasant. He lapsed into a lethargic state from which he could scarcely be roused at times. His parents were frightened. The doctors admitted they were helpless as they had no idea what was causing the illness. When it reached a critical stage they simply gave up all hope of saving his life.

Naturally the doctors in Gospic had no idea whatever about the true nature of Nikola's illness. Even medical science today knows nothing of "soul sickness" or the diseases which attack only disciples and not the average person. The individual himself, however, is usually able to supply the answer for he is under guidance from the Inner Planes. So after the Gospic doctors had given up hope for his life, and his parents had become somewhat resigned, Nikola turned to his books. He had been working in the local library at Gospic and had carried home an armful of selections just before his illness.

Listlessly he looked them over. He found one by Mark Twain. In it he suddenly discovered a paragraph which brought instant illumination. His enthusiasm for life was rekindled. The crisis passed. His health returned to normal. Nikola himself understood with profound conviction that it. was the writings of Mark Twain that had saved his life. He never forgot the incident to the end of his days and often spoke of his heartfelt gratitude to Mark Twain. Many years after the Gospic incident the two men met in New York and became very close friends. When Tesla himself had only a short time left on earth, and Mark Twain had been gone from the mortal scene for years, Tesla spoke of Mark coming to see him in his hotel room, and of their having a long visit together. When Tesla was reminded that Mark Twain had been dead for years, he vigorously denied it, adding that he was very much alive.

As indeed he is, even though invisible to certain people —the very same sort of people who fail to *see through* the humorous philosophy of Mark Twain, and into the supernal Light beyond. What did Mark and Nikola talk about in that memorable conversation which took place on a January day in 1943 in a New York hotel room, where Tesla's physical body lay breathing lightly in almost final readiness for departure?

Mark and Nikola were old friends, companions of ancient days in starry space. Like all such gentle humorists, like all such compassionate observers of human folly, like all old friends, they met on that occasion of joyous reunion, and they talked about the weather.

Standing there together in their magnificent clean bodies of vibrant light, it was only natural that their conversation should turn to that earlier sickroom scene in Gospic, when Nikola, with the vital help of high-frequency energies pouring from Mark's written words, had firmly set his course once again into an uncertain future among foolish mortals. It was Mark who had glimpsed the mortals in a humorous moment when they had reached an ebb point in their foolishness—a point where everybody talked about the weather, but nobody did anything about it.

That vibrant instant with Mark had set Nikola free from
his illness in Gospic. Nobody did anything about the weather,
Mark said. But Nikola joyfully remembered that he had
determined to do something about it years earlier when he
walked through a mountain thunderstorm. He was going to
learn to control lightning, and thereby control the weather.
He was the Somebody whose inventions would liberate and
illumine all the negative nobodies of the world.

Yes, that was what they talked about, the author and the
inventor, on a day in January, 1943.

The Gospic illness over, Nikola was ready to be guided to
his next necessary advancement. His father had been
thoroughly frightened and was now anxious to humor the
boy by permitting him to go to college at Carlstadt in Croa-
tia. Upon arriving in that city Nikola took up residence with
relatives, but his years in their home were unhappy ones. Almost at once he contracted malaria but he insisted upon starting his classes at the college.

His brilliance undimmed by either illness or lack of family
harmony, he completed the four-year college course in three
years. He carried away with him one lasting impression
which was to make everything easier in his life thereafter.
His professor of physics had held him enthralled with demon-
strations of feats performed with laboratory apparatus.
Tesla knew beyond a shadow of a doubt that his life was to
be fully and completely dedicated to a study of electricity.

With his life stretching complete before him, he returned
home, only to face up to the demands of the army. Again he
suddenly fell into a psychic illness. Again doctors gave up
all hope of saving his life. A cholera epidemic raged in the
town, and it was presumed that he had cholera in addition to

malaria, plus the nervous strain brought on by his college work, plus undernourishment resulting from the unhappy culinary situation in the home of his relatives in Carlstadt.

However, from the occult point of view Nikola suffered from a psychic illness in order to prevent a greater tragedy—compulsory military service. During the long illness which steadily became worse, Nikola's father became more and more frightened. The space people have not explained how much Nikola's father knew about the boy's origin. Of course, his mother had to know the details: but it is fairly clear that she herself was originally a Venusian. Perhaps the father was not, and it is even possible that Nikola was placed in the care of the mother without the father knowing of his origin. This all happened long ago in a remote mountain province. Women gave birth to children, often alone, or with only a midwife or neighbor in attendance. There are many possible explanations.

At any rate, whatever his understanding about his son, the Rev. Milutin Tesla was ready to accept anything to save the life of Nikola at a moment when the boy was drifting off into unconsciousness from which it seemed apparent he would not emerge. His father, in a firm, clear voice, commanded him not to die. In exchange, Nikola used his few remaining breaths to gasp out the news that he would remain if his father would let him become an electrical engineer. The bargain was struck on the instant, and within a matter of seconds vital energy began pouring through the tired body. In a few days Nikola was up and about and life was glorious once more.

The shadow of death had hovered close and then withdrawn. The shadow of the army loomed directly ahead. But Nikola's father had given his promise. Nikola was to be an

electrical engineer and the army was to be minus one recruit.
It was then that Nikola's father realized that his son needed
at least a year's vacation in the mountains in order to regain
not only his health but his freedom. Hurriedly Nikola was
provided with a hunting outfit, some books and papers. He
was gone before anyone in Gospic knew he had risen from
his deathbed.

In 1873 Nikola went to Gratz to study electrical engineering. He knew that the forces of destiny were shaping him
for a great purpose, and during his first year at Gratz he did
more than twice the amount of work required, passing all
examinations with the highest marks that could be awarded.
He hoped in this way to express his appreciation to his parents for saving him from army service and for permitting
him to study electrical engineering, but because they feared
he was again undermining his health they did not receive the
news of his high marks with joy.

During the second year he limited his studies to physics,
mathematics and mechanics in order to placate his parents.
Actually, however, he was guided in this decision by higher
forces, for it was important that he have plenty of leisure
time to devote to the next step in his unfoldment.

A piece of electrical equipment, a Gramme machine, that
could be used as either a dynamo or motor, had been acquired
by the Institute. It was a direct-current machine, and was
demonstrated to the class. It did not please Tesla because a
great deal of sparking took place at the commutator.

The professor explained that as long as electricity flowed

in one direction, a commutator would be necessary to change the direction, and the sparking could, therefore, not be avoided. Tesla replied that by using alternating current the commutator could be eliminated.

The professor was waiting for this suggestion and let loose a storm of criticism. He informed Tesla, in an abrupt and lofty professorial manner, that many men had already experimented with alternating current, and it was simply not feasible. In that instant Tesla had an intuitive flash. He knew the professor was wrong; he knew alternating current was possible; he knew that he would and could demonstrate it. The argument between the student and teacher went on during the remainder of the term, and although Tesla was unable to bring his vision down to practical results, he was by no means discouraged. The professor stated that Tesla's theories were contradicted by Nature and that settled the matter. It was far from settled in Tesla's mind.

The following year Tesla was to go to the University of Prague, but a lucrative position was offered him, so he saved his earnings, and enrolled at the university a year later. He extended his studies in physics and mathematics, but the vision of alternating current remained ever before him. In his heart he knew that he would make the great discovery that would elevate the infant science of electricity to the maturity of a great power.

Just after his graduation from the University of Prague his father died, and then Tesla set about to become self-supporting. The telephone invented by Alexander Graham Bell was making its advent in Europe at this time and in 1881 he was placed in charge of the new telephone exchange in Budapest. While there he developed an amplifier, which led to the present amplifiers on radio sets. He never patented the device, however, as his sole interest was still the problem of alternating current.

At this time, he underwent another severe psychic illness, during which his sense organs were affected by acute sensitivity. Apparently his vibrations were raised for some occult reason, and although doctors despaired of saving his life, he came through the period of suffering and his vibrations were restored to normal. But during the illness his dedication to the problem of alternating current had fully crystallized. He could scarcely think of anything else, and he knew that if he stopped working on it he would die: if he failed he would likewise perish.

He was a man without a choice, and on a late afternoon in February, 1882, he had recovered sufficiently to take a walk in a park in Budapest. His companion was a former classmate by the name of Szigeti. The two young men walked toward the setting sun. The skies ahead were painted with colors of high brilliance. Tesla was reciting aloud Goethe's *Faust*. It was a cosmic moment and Tesla was at one with the angels. Suddenly he stopped in a rigid pose. "Watch me," he cried out. "Watch me reverse it."

His startled companion was thrown into a state of panic, for Tesla seemed to be gazing at the sunset, and Szigeti feared that Tesla thought he could reverse the sun.

Szigeti suggested that they rest a moment, but Tesla talked on excitedly, looking steadily at something directly in front of him. Szigeti could see nothing, but Tesla was calling out in an exultant voice: "See how smoothly it runs. Now watch me stop it. Then start it. It goes just as smoothly in the opposite direction!"

Eventually Tesla became somewhat more composed and explained to his companion that he had just solved the probem of alternating current. He also revealed to Szigeti that e could see the motor before him, in full operation, and that e would not need to make drawings. But for the benefit of is friend who could see nothing but clear air in the spot where Tesla was operating his motor, they returned home together and talked far into the hours of the night, discussing very detail of the discovery.

Shortly thereafter Tesla was recommended for a job in Paris, and he was pleased to go to that city because it meant many contacts with Americans who were interested in all sorts of mechanical developments. Meanwhile he had mentally built a complete alternating-current system, both two-phase and three or more. His famous polyphase power system was a reality. As usual, he designed his dynamos, motors, transformers and all other devices in the fourth ether, performing his mathematical calculations on the etheric "blackboard" just as in his schooldays. He could test these mental constructs by leaving the machines in the ether to run for weeks. He would then examine them for signs of wear.

When he arrived in Paris he formulated a certain living pattern to which he adhered for the rest of his life, insofar as possible, or insofar as money would permit. He was always meticulously neat in dress, full of self-confidence, and carried himself with a poised, quiet attitude. For many years he had never rested more than five hours at night, and he claimed that he never slept more than two hours out of the five.

In Paris he would rise at five, swim in the Seine for half an hour, then dress and walk briskly for more than an hour to his place of work. He then ate a hearty breakfast, and by half-past eight he was ready for his duties. In the evening he would return to the center of Paris, dine at the best cafes, and contact any companions who were willing to listen to him describe his polyphase alternating current system.

At this point Tesla demonstrated that he was a world disciple, pledged to serve humanity and not a privileged group, for he never developed a secretive attitude about his inventions. He would gladly talk to anyone who would listen. He wanted only one thing—to give his invention to the human race so that all might benefit from it. He knew there was a fortune in it, but he was never concerned about the process of extracting fortunes from his machines.

He did not understand anything about money-making. This was due to the fact that he was a Venusian, and had not had any previous training in handling money. Money as we know it does not exist on Venus or anywhere in this solar system. The solar system operates on a basis of spiritual economy in which God's unlimited abundance and supply is accepted as Divine Law. A man-made money system such as exists on this planet is a direct contradiction of that Law. Further, the money system was created here as an instrument to serve the forces of darkness and has been used for the enslavement of humanity. Paul knew exactly what he was talking about when he stated that love of money was the root of all evil.

Tesla may have known nothing about money-making in the commercial shopping sense, but he had a deep understanding of the evils of the money system on this planet: In fact, his understanding in this regard was so profound that he never made the slightest attempt to come to terms with banking interests, because he realized that in doing so he would be coming to terms with the dark forces themselves. However, he was not going to take time out from his work to attempt to explain his attitude to anyone, so he just went ahead with his job of serving humanity and the Forces of

Light, and left others to serve the devil if they wished. Tesla was not a reformer. He was a transformer. His job was to transform the world from darkness to light. from enslavement to freedom.

Tesla made every effort to break down any secrecy surrounding his inventions. He was ready and willing to explain to all who would listen. There was no danger of his inventions being stolen at that time. In fact he could not even give them away. The forces of darkness were already securely entrenched in the electrical field. They wanted no part of any invention designed by a White Magician. Well they knew that if Tesla ever invaded the electrical field in global fashion it would mark the end of the old way of life with all its international complexities—its evil money system, its corrupt political delusions, its churchianity, its educational inadequacies.

There remained nearly twenty years until the turn of the century, and yet Tesla stood as the great colossus, the mighty genius who, working hand-in-hand with his Creator, might have saved the world from further violence of clashing forces of evil. Years later, when alternating current was finally adopted in America through the good offices of George Westinghouse. the dark forces still fought to turn the tide against Tesla. Finally they capitulated and took the opposite stand. They supported the adoption of alternating current and its widespread use, but only when they found that Tesla had outwitted them by obsoleting his own invention. He abandoned the whole system set up around the distribution of electricity by wires and developed a World Wireless System whereby everyone could have all the electricity they wished by merely attaching a small antenna to home, shop or office building.

The forces of darkness would have none of this and to this day, in 1958, they have been successful in preventing the wireless system from reaching the attention of the public which would demand its use. But now Tesla, working in the scientific department of Shamballa, has again had the last word to say through his disciple, Otis T. Carr of Baltimore. As the New Age advances it is quite likely that Tesla's wireless system for electrical distribution may be obsoleted by Carr's free-energy devices. And so it is that the Legions of Light move steadily on to Victory.

As the new civilization takes shape it will be clearly seen that Tesla had access to no secrets at any time. He had direct contact with Universal Truth. Tesla worked out ways and means to anchor Truth on the physical plane through using physical matter. The early Root Races on the planet worked in exactly the same manner. They brought down and anchored in physical matter the higher vibrations direct from the Godhead. Matter is spirit slowed down; spirit is matter speeded up. All is One.

The anchoring of Truth, or the lowering of vibrations, has never been a secret process. It has always been part of the teachings of the Ageless Wisdom. But it is a well-known fact that you can't get Truth out of a man if he has no available Truth in him. Truth is Light. Light which is imprisoned or obscured cannot illumine a person. Only the individual with a clean atomic structure, or one who understands and practices transmutation, can hope to anchor Truth in physical matter. The average scientists, especially those contaminated by working with military weapons, are in no position to embark on a search for Truth. It will not be found in an H-bomb.

When Tesla agreed to undertake the task of bringing light

to the earth he envisioned this globe as one vast terrestrial lamp spiralling through the skies toward its God-ordained destiny of perfected evolution: bearing upon its lighted body a race of Illumined Initiates, freed from the cycle of rebirth, journeying back to their Source, to their appointed mansion in the Father's House.

This was Tesla's great secret, if secret he had. Let those who feel overlooked because they were not called upon to share it, ask themselves at this point if they are sure they are quite ready, even now, to share it. Or are they like those disciples of Jesus who had to listen to the Master tell them they were not ready to share the knowledge of certain things: that to speak of such Truths would place upon them a greater burden of Light than they could bear.

Tesla's life in Paris went on smoothly. He enjoyed robust health. But he was employed by the Continental Edison Company, working all day on direct-current machines, and this proved to be an irksome point. His superior alternating-current inventions, although still in the fourth ether, were tauntingly close at hand.

Finally the situation was changed abruptly by an accident in the railway station at Strassburg in Alsace, where an Edison powerhouse and electric lights had been installed. Alsace then belonged to Germany and the electrical installation was formally opened with Emperor William I present. Unfortunately, when the lights were turned on the glory was indeed brief, for a short circuit caused an entire wall of the railway station to be blown to bits.

Tesla was sent from Paris to Strassburg to survey the damage and proceed with repairs. Once the work got under way and he could serve in a supervisory capacity, he arranged for space and tools in a nearby machine shop, and there he proceeded to transfer his dream of alternating current from the fourth ether to the physical plane.

He was an amateur machinist but a meticulous worker, and gradually a large collection of miscellaneous parts of a two-phase alternating-current motor took shape in the machine shop. Tesla not only made each part exact to a thousandth of an inch but he carefully polished it to make it more exact. He had no working drawings or blueprints. He formed each part from metal to exactly match the etheric part which he saw before him.

He did not have to test the parts because he knew they would fit. When he had finished the entire collection he quickly assembled the machine and started up his power generator. The cosmic moment had struck. He closed the switch. The armature of his motor turned, built up speed. He closed the reversing switch. The armature stood still, then instantly started turning in the opposite direction.

Alternating current had been transferred from the invisible to the visible, from the fourth ether to the dense physical plane, from a substance lighter than gas to metal.

So there in the noisy machine shop in Strassburg stood the very motor which Tesla had first discovered in the sunset glow in the park at Budapest, walking with his friend, Szigeti. Even the beautiful lines from Goethe's *Faust*, which he had been proclaiming aloud as he walked, were still appropriate:

> The glow retreats, done is the day of toil;
> It yonder hastes, new fields of life exploring;
> Ah, that no wing can lift me from the soil,
> Upon its track to follow, follow soaring. . . .

Tesla's unique method of constructing his first motor gives an excellent clue to the manner in which all Initiates consciously work, although they usually precipitate the etheric form instantly into physical matter, without intermediary construction work. They can externalize whatever they need by first visualizing it in the ethers, then calling it forth into physical density.

That is why spaceships are described as being constructed without rivets, welding, seams, or cracks around doors. They are not constructed but precipitated direct from the ether.

Since the laggards came and human beings forgot how to precipitate what they need, all man-made forms are first created in mental matter by a designer thinking through his problem and creating a thoughtform. Mental matter is on the same plane as gas, and is, therefore, one density lower than the fourth ether. But mental matter is all that the average person can manipulate, and is not by any means pure but is heavily weighted with astral accumulations. It is virtually impossible for the average person to create a clear, precise thoughtform, free from personal emotional distortions. Since he cannot control his mental constructs with any degree of success, his matrix or thoughtform is often composed more of fantasy than of fact. When it is lowered into form the physical plane result is often useless, ugly, and a spiritual monstrosity.

In the summer of 1884, shortly after Tesla returned from Strassburg to Paris, he arrived in New York City with exactly four cents in his pocket, and a book of his poems. In addition, he had a letter of introduction to Thomas A. Edison.

In a few brief weeks in Europe many things had happened to force this hurried and unplanned voyage to America. While Tesla was still in Strassburg he tried to interest business men there in his new alternating-current motor which he had·built from the parts he had made by hand. He could not stir up a spark of enthusiasm for the machine which was later to revolutionize the electrical industry of the world. Then, when he returned to Paris to collect the substantial fee which he had been promised for getting the Strassburg installation in operation, the company conveniently failed to remember anything about the arrangement. One official however, did suggest to Tesla that he go direct to Mr. Edison in America.

Within a few days Tesla sold his personal belongings, packed his bags, and bought his railroad and steamship tickets. However, just as he was about to board the train to take him from Paris to the ship he discovered he had been robbed. He ran along the moving train and boarded it, paying his fare with loose change and notes he had in his pockets after his wallet was stolen. He also boarded the ship, explaining that his ticket had been stolen. Fortunately, no one showed up to claim his reservations, so he was allowed to continue on his way to the United States. Without luggage and with only a few cents in change, he finally landed in New York.

He lacked fare for either cab or trolley, so he set out to walk from the pier to the home of a friend, for he.had fortunately retained his address book. He walked past an electrical repair shop and inside he saw a weary and obviously harrassed workman struggling to repair a machine.

He entered the shop. "Let me repair it," he said to the mechanic. The workman, without further inquiry, permitted Tesla to set to work. Although the task was difficult Tesla finally had the machine operating. The grateful mechanic handed him twenty dollars and offered him a steady job. But

Tesla thanked him, explaining that he was on his way to another job, and could not accept his offer.

He continued on his way, found his friend, and remained at his home overnight. The next morning he set out to call on Mr. Edison who then had headquarters in New York on South Fifth Avenue, a street which later became known as West Broadway.

The meeting between the two men was not auspicious. Edison belonged to the direct-current school of thought, and Tesla was not only in opposition to direct current, but was actually the inventor of alternating current. Furthermore, Edison was lacking in technical education. He was totally unable to understand Tesla's ability to visualize a problem in its entirety without doing any mechanical work on it or following the usual trial-and-error method.

Yet Edison was conscious of Tesla's great value, and while he could not afford to hire him as a competitor of the direct-current method, yet he could not afford to let it be known that he had not hired him. Rather grudgingly he employed Tesla, and almost at once Edison was placed in a position from which only the incomparable Tesla could rescue him.

The finest passenger ship of the day was called the Oregon. Edison had installed one of his electric light plants on the steamship and the vessel was ready to set sail. However, the lighting plant failed completely, and Edison was unable to find the cause of the difficulty. Tesla was dispatched to the ship late one afternoon and by the following morning had the dynamos functioning perfectly.

This incident served to advance his prestige with Edison. When he later approached Edison with a plan to improve the design of the Edison dynamos and at the same time lower the operating cost, Edison not only agreed but offered Tesla a fee of $50,000 if the work came up to expectations.

Tesla labored at the task for many months, putting in many hours of overtime daily. He completed designs for twenty-four types of dynamos.

Some of the machines were built and tested and proved to be very satisfactory. Patents were taken out by Edison. When the entire job was finished, Tesla requested the $50,-000 which he had been promised. Edison, however, claimed that the agreement had been merely a "joke", whereupon Tesla resigned his job immediately. The Strassburg incident had been repeated.

It was the year of 1885. Had Tesla known the heartaches that lay ahead he might not have had the courage to continue his efforts to provide alternating current for a world that seemed to offer him nothing but scorn. Looking back over Tesla's entire life it can be seen that he never capitulated to the evil money system which prevails on this planet. Again and again, just as he was about to grasp and use the contaminated medium of exchange, it was snatched from him. This left Tesla free, but the karma engendered descended upon humanity.

Even today, fifteen years after Tesla's death, humanity still awaits the superman's great inventions which could give untold comfort to physical plane existence. And the reason? —a lack of funds adequate to develop the inventions on a world-wide scale. Tesla would settle for nothing short of global operations, bringing help to all the peoples of the earth. It is very significant that he wished to encompass the planet with his work, and in the case of the interplanetary communications set, the solar-system. Being a Venusian he could not produce inventions that would remain earthbound. The superman was restless to grasp the extended hand of interplanetary friendship; to prepare the Dark Star of earth for its great cosmic initiation into solar freedom.

But in 1885 the financial world was not ready to give up its evil interests in the Dark Star. It perhaps is even less ready today, but today the Christ Forces have all dark manipulators on the run, and happily for humanity, it will be the last run. The Forces of Light are now able to stand firmly on the side of humanity and fight evil to a finish.

In 1885 financial matters were handled with shrewdness and cunning. Honesty was easily set aside by the fortune-makers of the day. At this time a group of promoters offered to finance a small company to promote Tesla. They were to pay him a modest salary and were to reward him on a grand scale with stock in the company. He thought he saw an opportunity to develop alternating current, but once the company had been formed Tesla was obliged to develop an arc light for street and factory illumination. It was to be a type of light 'which the promoters could use to further certain schemes of expansion.

The light was developed and Tesla took out patents on his design. However, the company had been organized in such a tricky manner that when Tesla was awarded his stock he soon found it to be worthless. The promoters prospered and Tesla was left without funds.

He then struck bottom in his American venture, for by the year of 1887 he was actually forced to dig ditches and take other laboring jobs at $2 a day. But even this provided the ladder on which he climbed to success, for the foreman in charge of the ditch digging recognized Tesla as a man of genius. He introduced him to Mr. A. K. Brown of the Western Union Telegraph Company. Mr. Brown, in turn, interested a friend in Tesla. The two men put up sufficient money to finance the Tesla Electric Company.

In April of 1887, Tesla opened his own laboratory and workshop on South Fifth Avenue, now West Broadway, and found himself a neighbor of Edison. Edison had turned down Tesla's idea for alternating current, striving to boost the prestige of direct current. Yet, in the end, Tesla won the competitive fight, despite the fact that he was backed by limited funds while Edison was financed by J. P. Morgan.

Tesla's hour had struck and ever thereafter the Dark Star was to be illumined by his incomparable genius.

It is impossible, even today, to evaluate the virgin field of electrical science which Tesla explored within a few months after his new laboratory was opened. The United States Patent Office could not easily grasp the scope of his work. They considered his inventions so original and so basic that they simply started issuing a succession of patents that brought the new age of power to birth in one mighty surge of advancement.

The entire electrical world of 1887 was engulfed by the sweeping new advance. It can now be seen in retrospect that in the seventy years which have since elapsed, civilization has not yet absorbed even the basic fundamental scientific achievements produced by Tesla. As for the philosophy of Tesla, it is hardly known that he had anything to offer in that field, as perhaps he did not—for his philosophy had already been presented by Jesus. Since western minds had failed to grasp even the basic teachings offered down

through the countless centuries by the Hierarchy, and then
had ignored the true meanings underlying the work of
Jesus, it is abundantly clear why Tesla did not bother to
waste his time tossing pearls.

Within six months after Tesla opened his laboratory in
1887, he applied to the Patent Office for a single patent
covering his entire electrical system which he had designed
at that time. The Patent Office was overwhelmed by this
"package deal" and insisted that Tesla break his single
patent down into seven parts. This was done and in April
of 1888 he applied for five more patents which were granted.
Toward the end of 1888 he was issued eighteen additional
patents.

By this time the entire scientific world was not only
amazed, but completely baffled by the sudden manner in
which their cherished concepts were swept away over night.
It was not easy to make such a quick and monumental ad-
justment to new values, especially in view of the fact that
many of the scientists and technicians of the day, then as
now, prided themselves on being strong-minded, free-think-
ing men who were capable of standing on their two feet and
meeting the issues of the day.

They also prided themselves on being God-fearing men,
independent men, who, if they wished to invent a machine,
could do so without calling upon the aid of the Creator.
But in some mysterious fashion the Creator had somehow
got back on the job through Tesla. So these God-fearing
men looked everywhere for the answer except in the right
place. For a man who fears God can never love Him, and a
man who places God on a pedestal high in the sky is most
certainly in fear of Him. The only way to love God is to
bring His energy down into dense matter by lowering the

vibration, and then anchor it there. The early Root Races had the answer as did Tesla.

The social gossips of the day back in 1888 also had their word to say about Tesla. To them he was at once the most fascinating and the most aggravating of men. He did not share their interests, and they could not seem to find a way of sharing his. It was incomprehensible to them that a man of such cosmopolitan tastes could overlook them so completely, so utterly. So far as women were concerned Tesla was considered to be the world's most eligible bachelor. Ambitious mothers and anxious daughters hovered close, or at least let us say they tried. But no one ever got close to Tesla. So far as men were concerned, Tesla was constantly inventing machines which could be manufactured and sold. This stamped the sign of the dollar indelibly upon him. Over the years the Tesla-marriage-money subject became a topic of international conversation.

The next momentous Tesla development came on May 16, 1888 when, in response to an invitation, he gave a lecture and demonstration before the American Institute of Electrical Engineers. This lecture served notice upon the entire world that the greatest genius of the age had brought his discoveries to fruition, presenting civilization with alternating current, and thus setting electricity geographically free. Under Edison's direct current system it was necessary to have a powerhouse in the center of every square-mile, or even closer in large cities. This presented an impossible situation if electricity was to become a planetary source of power as Tesla visualized.

Tesla had no desire to develop his inventions commercially, for he preferred to spend his time in research. He knew that the very inventions which he was in the process of patenting would become obsolete in a short time if he could continue his research. Edison fought resolutely to maintain the prestige of direct current, for he had invented the incandescent electric lamp, and in order to sell the lamps he had to make electricity available so that the lamps could be used. Moreover, Edison's financial interests were tied completely to those of J. P. Morgan, and Edison was not free to pursue any course except the strictly commercial one.

When Tesla gave his famous lecture on May 16, 1888, George Westinghouse of Pittsburgh was in the audience. Westinghouse was already well known as the inventor of an air brake for trains and of many other electrical devices. He had made a fortune in exploiting his own inventions. He was a man of tremendous vision and he immediately recognized the vast possibilities, commercially and geographically, of Tesla's alternating current system. Shortly thereafter he contacted Tesla for an interview. In a matter of minutes Westinghouse agreed to pay Tesla one million dollars outright for the alternating current patents, plus a royalty of one dollar per horsepower.

It was Westinghouse, therefore, who seized the opportunity to develop Tesla's patents which would supply electricity to the entire world. In the few moments required to negotiate the deal, a friendship was formed between the two men which, in its magnificence and trust, was of transcendent beauty. As things worked out, the friendship was almost the only happy development that resulted from the meeting, but as the years passed Tesla never betrayed the slightest bitterness or regret over misfortunes that came to both of them as a result of their cooperation.

Tesla spent a useless, weary year in Pittsburgh attempting

to get Westinghouse launched in his manufacturing efforts,
but finally refused to remain longer. The Westinghouse engineers, accustomed to their own way of doing things, were
baffled and confused by Tesla's magic. Tesla in turn had
no way of communicating with the men since he could not
get down to their level of understanding. Tesla was a great
teacher of philosophy to certain individuals. He was also
a great teacher of what might be called cosmic engineering—
again to certain individuals. But he selected these individuals
personally. They were disciples, but they were already active
disciples for the Forces of Light.

To expect Tesla to go into a manufacturing plant and
teach a group of American engineers at all stages of evolutionary development was, of course, ridiculous. But perhaps
even Tesla did not realize the scope of his own greatness,
and the intellectual gap which existed as a barrier between
him and those of earth who had not yet attained discipleship. At any rate, after his departure from the Pittsburgh
plant, the Westinghouse engineers worked out their own
problems, and eventually the manufacturing process got
under way.

Tesla returned to his own laboratory in New York, to
his beloved research—a wealthy man, free from the need
for commercialism. This freedom was for him the greatest
triumph that might come to a human soul. Working again
on research for his polyphase power system, he was granted
forty-five patents in this country during the next four years,
in addition to more than a hundred in foreign countries.

Edison had long been busy aiming competitive lances in all directions. He was strictly a commercial money-making man. He was untrained in the science of electrical engineering and, therefore, had to depend upon those whose services he could get for hire. He was tied, hand and foot, to the value of the dollar and was thereby forced into the role of a huckster. He could never shake himself free from the clutches of the monkey on his back in the form of the J. P. Morgan interests, although there is no evidence to show that he desired to do so. Some men are destined to play the role of the organ-grinder. It does not lie within the karmic patterns of all men to compose great music.

Edison had tangled with Westinghouse on many occasions. But when it was discovered that Westinghouse, capable and far-visioned, a successful inventor and a successful business man, had taken on the task of developing Tesla's alternating current, the battle took on a new and fiercer phase. It was at this time that the New York State Prison authorities stepped openly into the White Magic field of electricity, and turned it into a field of black magic almost overnight. They adopted alternating current as developed by Tesla for the electrocution of condemned prisoners.

Tesla claimed that the Edison interests had engineered the project to discredit alternating current. There was more than a little truth in this, although that was probably not the original purpose. For the Edison interests, anxious to make a dollar even one jump ahead of the undertaker, had tried to provide direct current to power the electric chair. But they had failed, because the plain fact of the matter was that direct current could not be produced at the high voltages required. All this was lost on the public, however, as the

Edison interests proclaimed from the housetops that the prison's choice of current was proof of the deadly danger of Tesla's invention.

Now we can look back and realize that this victory of the forces of darkness, operating from the astral plane directly through the prison authorities, touched off a retrogressive movement which has since carried certain aspects of civilization back to evil days which have not been known on this planet since the sinking of Atlantis.

Now people like to look back to the pre-atomic age, and blame the nuclear scientists for the present destructive threat to humanity. But nuclear scientists would not have had a ghost of a chance of exercising their black magic, had not the road to darkness been well paved already by black magicians long in control on the astral plane. The New York State Prison authorities cooperated to the hilt in assisting the black magicians to take over control of the alternating-current invention and all humanity has suffered by being robbed, and robbed, and robbed of the true advantages of the invention since that dreadful day.

The control by black magicians and their tools has since been broken on the Inner Planes, and even the tools will soon be eliminated from the physical plane. The Christ Forces, assisted by the angelic kingdom, have seized and removed all black magicians from the planet. Their human tools still exist on the physical plane, by the thousands, but their nefarious endeavors will be smashed down as soon as the seventh Ray has done a bit more of its beneficent work of transmutation.

While New York State Prison authorities were busying themselves in an all-out effort to lower the planetary vibrations by using electricity, the Third Aspect of God, or the

Holy Spirit, to electrocute condemned prisoners, George Westinghouse prepared to use the Tesla invention of alternating current to put the entire United States on an electrical power basis. Tesla, meanwhile, back at his research, set about to make obsolete his earlier inventions, and place the entire world on one simple electrical system which would enable all of God's children, from the Arctic to the Antarctic, to have light—more abundant light and living advantages.

The year had turned to 1891. Tesla and Westinghouse were firmly aligned with the Divine Plan and their combined energies were enabling a tiny portion of this Plan to manifest. But where there is Light-in-Action on this Dark Star, it is always consuming darkness. In other words, there has not yet come a time when we could say that we had a safe dividend of light left over for intelligent, constructive uses. Every unit of light released by disciples on this planet must still be used to illumine the suffering atoms wherein evil is bottled up in the form of astral debris.

In 1891 the karma that was being engendered by the New York State Prison authorities alone, was so dense in its accumulation that the forces of darkness were enabled to sweep into the alternating-current field without hindrance. The black leaders were reinforced by a vast horde of disembodied criminals from the astral plane, bent on vengeance. They struck savagely at Westinghouse, for his company alone would supply the nation with alternating current, providing great wealth to Tesla for years to come in the form of horsepower royalties.

The dense overshadowing of the Westinghouse financial advisors commenced. In those days little was known about astral influences, and when the deluded, bewitched money-men went into a panic, they merely thought they were being

astute financial wizards. Here was a picture of little big-
shots, utterly dazzled by the mocking brilliance of their own
arrogance.

A number of quick mergers with smaller companies took
place and a new unit was formed, known as the Westinghouse Electric and Manufacturing Company. But before this
deal was finalized, the financial group put George Westinghouse on the spot, and told him that he was to destroy his
contract with Tesla. The alternative? The money-men would
destroy the Weshinghouse organization as it existed at that
time.

The financial wizards were crazed by their astral overshadowing, and goaded into a greedy desire to consume
all. They were adamant in their determination to share no
profits with anyone—not even with the goose Tesla, who had
laid the golden egg. Against this mighty army of darkness,
George Westinghouse stood out like a giant pillar of light—
but a lone giant. The financial interests were set to see the
company destroyed rather than yield a single dollar in horsepower royalty to Tesla.

But even one on the side of the Forces of Light is in itself
a victorious majority against evil. Westinghouse firmly
grasped the scales of justice, and he went direct to Tesla
and humbly told the story of his seeming defeat. Tesla quickly turned it into a spiritual triumph that will ring down
through the years as a cosmic moment in which two men
touched divinity.

Standing there before Westinghouse, Tesla smiled serenely
and tore up his contract without a trace of bitterness. At
that moment he was entitled to at least twelve million dollars in royalties, but he tossed the scraps of his contract into
the wastebasket. He had saved the Westinghouse organiza-

tion, and Westinghouse would give his polyphase system to the world. The bankers could satisfy their love for money. Today this unfortunate planet is still reaping the black harvest from the seeds scattered far and wide by the bewitched money-men.

It has been said often that failure to pay horsepower royalties to Tesla proved to be the greatest handicap to scientific and industrial progress which the human race has ever experienced on this globe. In this year of 1958 the United States and all allied nations of the world are wondering why scientific superiority has been lost in recent years. The answer is simple. The pattern of events is not difficult to trace.

Karmic law was set in motion by the New York State Prison using Tesla's alternating-current invention to electrocute condemned prisoners. The karmic debt thus incurred precipitated at the point where alternating-current development was centered. Tesla was a White Magician and was protected against direct attack by the dark forces. He could be reached only indirectly. But the Westinghouse organization, through its money system, was wide open. The dark forces were able to attack freely through that open channel. This imperiled the work of Tesla. But since it was society that connived to support the prison authorities in their nefarious work, it is society that has had to suffer the karmic results. America allowed the Tesla inventions to be mis-used. It is America that must pay the karmic debt through a decline in scientific achievement.

A very few years after Tesla and Westinghouse made their historic decision, Tesla was a global intellectual giant of such stature that he could easily, with the use of his inventions and discoveries, have swung this planet from evil to goodness, from darkness to light, from ignorance to illumination. But society, in its utter complacency, preferred prison methods to the methods of a Venusian Initiate. And so the mills of the gods continued to grind slowly, awaiting the incoming seventh Ray which would bring the cleansing Violet Fire of transmutation to the Dark Star.

After the financial setback engineered by the Westinghouse money-men, Tesla never again had suffcient funds to develop his inventions. On many occasions his co-workers begged him to develop some small aspect of his inventions in order to make money to support his greater discoveries, but Tesla always refused to spend his time on what he termed small stuff. He had no desire to benefit a few people. He desired only to benefit humanity. Some of his co-workers felt that he was just being stubborn, but Tesla wisely knew his proper course.

It must be remembered that another great Initiate by the name of Jesus also tried to sell society on the idea of a better world. In this year of 1958 Jesus is still patiently waiting for the majority to join the minority in the support of His efforts. Tesla was well acquainted with the work of Jesus, and with the work of hundreds of other Initiates who had made supreme sacrifices for a belligerent and ungrateful humanity. Sanat Kumara waited nineteen million years for the prodigal sons of earth to grow weary of consuming their husks. Intuitively Tesla knew that he, too, could await the day of man's great awakening.

When Tesla was nearly eighty years of age he was asked to give a speech before the Institute of Immigrant Welfare which, at a dinner meeting at the Hotel Biltmore on May 12, 1938, was to present the great inventor with an honorary citation. Tesla wrote out a speech which was read at the dinner because he did not feel equal to attending in person. He had not only survived through many, many years of extreme poverty, but he had been ridiculed for failing to commercialize his inventions. He was often unable to pay his hotel bills, and was forced to move frequently, leaving his luggage until friends could assist him to get settled in another lodging place.

Yet with this spectre of poverty always dogging at his heels, he gazed without rancor at a world which had waxed wealthy out of the power he had made available. And so on the occasion of the Biltmore dinner he paid tribute to Westinghouse in a magnificent testimonial to the heartfelt friendship which had always existed between the two men:

"George Westinghouse was, in my opinion, the only man on this globe who could take my alternating-current system under the circumstances then existing and win the battle against prejudice and money power. He was a pioneer of imposing stature, one of the world's true noblemen of whom America may well be proud and to whom humanity owes an immense debt of gratitude."

So it was at the age of 80 years that Tesla, the only man on the globe who could have invented alternating current, cited George Westinghouse as the only man on the Dark Star who could have developed it in spite of the pitiless and ruthless attacks by the forces of darkness, entrenched behind the money screen within his own company. Tesla declared his position as an Initiate in this statement about his friend, just as surely as did another Initiate who entered into the Temple and flayed the money-lenders with a whip.

As a Venusian Tesla was not karmically obliged to deal with money-lenders. His magnificent gesture of tearing up his own contract with Westinghouse showed that as a

Venusian he was willing to go to any length to help his friend, knowing full well that Westinghouse was shouldering for all humanity a karmic burden so great that he could scarcely bear up under it. With the aid of Tesla's warm and enduring friendship he did bear up, giving Tesla's polyphase system to the world, thus eliminating a vast part of society's karmic debt. Tesla voiced a divine pronouncement when he stated that George Westinghouse was one of the world's true noblemen.

During the final years of his life, as he neared the age of 80, Tesla was aided by a $7,200 annual honorarium paid to him by the Yugoslav Government on behalf of the Tesla Institute at Belgrade. As the hour of Tesla's birth approached, the spaceship on which he was born neared the earth in a mountain province that is now part of Yugoslavia. As the hour of his death approached, it was Yugoslavia that honored him and supported him financially.

The Tesla Institute was opened in Belgrade in 1936, in commemoration of Tesla's eightieth birthday. Formal celebrations were held throughout the country over a period of a week, honoring the greatest national hero the Yugoslavs had ever known. The Tesla Institute, endowed by both government and private sources, was equipped with a splendid research laboratory and library. Every bit of writing or information that had any bearing on Tesla and his inventions was collected and made available to research students at the Institute. American students have been deprived of any opportunity to learn about Tesla because his name is seldom mentioned in school books, even science textbooks.

In the United States, the nation which Tesla had honored with his citizenship, and the point from which his great inventions had rayed forth like light from a central sun. Tesla passed his eightieth birthday quietly. He was interviewed and questioned about his World Wireless System for electrical distribution, a system which he had perfected many years before, and which rendered his polyphase system obsolete. He showed not the slightest sign of resentment over the fact that billions upon billions of dollars had been wasted by promoters in a greedy effort to extract the last penny of profit from an electrical system that was as outmoded as a dinosaur.

Tesla was comforted by his own inner joyous knowledge that he had not been called to share in commercial exploitations that needlessly sapped the wealth of the world. His philosophy of brotherhood, of friendship toward humanity, of gratitude toward his Creator, never wavered. And so he said, when questioned about his World Wireless Power System:

"Perhaps I was a little premature. We can get along without it as long as my polyphase system continues to meet our needs. Just as soon as the need arises, however, I have the system ready to be used with complete success."

It is still ready and it is still waiting to be used. Promoters are still withholding from the public the knowledge that such a system exists as an invention, waiting to be used. Promoters are still seeking to expand Tesla's obsolete polyphase system throughout the world, burdening the earth with miles upon miles of needless cables, conduits, wires and posts, providing dangerous playthings for high winds and blizzards. But this is the greedy method by which fortunes are made at the expense of the public.

In the New Age only new age methods will be utilized. Very soon now will come the big planetary housecleaning.

Then down will come all the cables, conduits, wires and posts, which the public is now paying to have installed. What fools these mortals be!

Since Otis T. Carr has now come forth with his free-energy devices it is quite probable that Tesla, working from Shamballa, has in mind a system that will obsolete the World Wireless System. But at any rate, as Tesla said on his eightieth birthday, the system is there, waiting to be used with complete success if needed.

It calls for a small antenna device to be attached atop every house, office building, shop and factory. This device will enable the occupants of the building to have all the electricity they need without meters or wirings. The antenna will pick up a beamed supply of current, just as a radio picks up a broadcasted program. Inside the home or building the electrical service units such as lights, irons, stoves, adding machines, typewriters, and so forth, will be free from wires and plugs for wall outlets. The units will pick up the necessary current beamed from the antenna.

Even when Tesla had his old laboratories on South Main Street (now West Broadway) in New York, he had lights which could be picked up and placed in any position anywhere in the laboratory, wherever light happened to be needed at the moment. His lights were merely glass tubes, free from wires and wall fixtures.

So the inventor, for many years, enjoyed the fruits of his own inventions, while the public has paid and paid and paid the pipers who ever pipe for more money profits from their outmoded merchandise.

The Tesla wireless method for electrical distribution is a gift which the world might have utilized for the past half century had the public demanded it. But an uninformed public is a silent public. The public gets its information largely from newspapers and magazines, radio and TV. These sources are, in turn, controlled and censored by their advertisers and government secret-guarders. This conditioned public then dictates to its teachers and its preachers, telling them what to teach and what pulpit topics would be most uplifting to the community spirit. Thus the vicious circle whirls round and round like a sputnik.

Even Tesla himself was told off by J. P. Morgan when he explained his world wireless system to the financier. Morgan listened to Tesla describe the glories of his invention, and then the money baron dismissed the whole subject as impractical because, as he pointed out, there would be no way of making money off the people if the people could have as much electricity as they wished by merely putting up a little antenna on their homes, or factories or office buildings.

Morgan further reminded Tesla that under the present system the manufacturers of wires, poles, and electrical installation equipment of all kinds, could make fortunes, and in addition, the electricity could be metered and everybody could be charged for every kilowat they used. Tesla pointed out that electricity was free in the atmosphere, a free gift of God to His people, but such idealism naturally could not penetrate the thinking of a financier.

Early in the years when Tesla was training Otis T. Carr, he called Carr's attention to the same fact—electricity is free in the atmosphere, a gift of God to His people. Carr agreed with Tesla instantly. But Carr was not a financier. He was merely working as a clerk in a hotel package room. Perhaps therein lies the answer.

This is the end of this publication.

Any remaining blank pages are for our book binding
requirements and are blank on purpose.

To search thousands of interesting publications like this one,
please remember to visit our website at:

http://www.kessinger.net

CPSIA information can be obtained
at www.ICGtesting.com
Printed in the USA
BVHW011116090521
606887BV00009B/345